HOW A SUSTAINABLE PALM OIL INDUSTRY CAN ACCOMPANY CAMEROON IN ATTAINING ITS VISION 2035

Preface

Inspired by a simple but heart touching email from an origin of the Ndian Division of the South West Region residing in the United States of America in which he was responding to certain claims of adverse social and environmental effects related to the creation of an oil palm plantation in his division.

He said and I quote *"Have you ever lived without running water or clean drinking water? Have you ever lived in a place where it takes 2 days or more to cover a distance of 50 miles, just to get to your village? A place where the roads are so bad, hard working farmers can't get their perishable goods to the market on time? Do you know what it means to be enrolled in a primary or secondary school with no classrooms, benches, teachers, books, computers, roads, health care, electricity, dormitories, etc? Do you understand what it means to see a loved one die because of lack of access to affordable health care? What is the per capita income of population in the region? What is the infant mortality rate in the region?"* End of quote.

I thought it wouldn't be honest if I didn't share information to the public on how the establishment of an oil palm plantation in his division could contribute in answering some of his worries.

Permit me quote the Director of Environmental Conservation, Department of the State of Sabah in Malaysia, I quote.

"Oil palm cultivation is one of the main economic activities of the state, which not only effect extensive land development but also provides substantial revenue to the state as well as the nation as a whole. It is also one of the pivotal aspects that acts as the catalyst for regional infrastructural development, particularly road network within interior areas".

Information in this book is drawn both from my empirical and scientific background as one of those who grew up in the heart of an oil palm plantation, who has served in the biggest oil palm plantations in the world and who has spent all his life working on oil palm. The information in this book is not only pragmatic but it is also coherent with situations in some countries extensively cited in this book. The arguments in this book are based on experience obtained during my seven years stay in Indonesia and Malaysia. These arguments are also drawn from the wealth of scientific understanding that I have gathered in universities across the continents.

The issues raised in this book are related to socio economic development, and not only development *per se* but sustainable development.

Permit me to quote again a respectable African Statesman **The Honourable Alhadji Sir Abubakar Tafawa Balewa, KBE**, former Prime

Minister of Nigeria at the time when Southern Cameroons were jointly administered with Eastern Nigeria.

"Many of you will remember that in 1955, the Cameroons Development Corporation ran into difficulties. The Southern Cameroons Government depended on that Corporation for most of its revenue and if the revenue from the Corporation fell below £580,000 a year, the Government itself would be in difficulty"

Income is supposed to be generated and not expected to fall from the sky. Income is obtained if there is production of goods and services in the economy. A country is less developed, emerging or developed based on socio economic criteria, whose foundation can be traced to the production of goods and services or business. It would be very strategic for any country to capitalise on its comparative advantages in order to have a place in the provision of goods and services in the world market.

Today, Cameroon cannot compete with China or other Asian nations in the domain of electronics and ICTs. There are no production industriues for computers, cell phones and other minor electrical appliances in Cameroon. Cameroon is therefore doomed to import all of these as of now. However, Cameroon has a comparative advantage on some of the major agricultural products that can enable it push export revenue and reverse balance deficit. For example, Cameroon can reverse its balance deficit in 10 years time by stopping palm oil imports. This may take shorter time (2 years) if Cameroon exports part of its projected production as outlined in this book. It is worthy to note that Cameroon imported oil palm from Gabon and Liberia in the course of 2016.

The cultivation of oil palm is dependent on many natural resources, human resources and ecological processes that interlink them. Oil palm cultivation necessitates good soils, appropriate climatic conditions, water resources and manpower, and since few trees are planted per hectare (143/ha), companies need vast expanses of land. The use of vast areas of land for the cultivation of oil palm should not lead to the destruction of ecological niches and human settlement. This is the new strategy for sustainable oil palm plantation establishments.

Cameroon is yet to exploit 0.05% of its land area suitable for the cultivation of oil palm. At present, Cameroon is yet to cover 400 000 ha of land for oil palm cultivation out of the total area of 8.3 million ha of suitable land. Ivory Coast, Gabon and Liberia are the only self-sufficient producers of palm oil in Africa. The other countries are net importers of palm oil. A country like the Central African Republic has got a negative growth rate of the industry (-0.6%) and the area under oil palm, as a fraction of their suitable land is 0.002%. Slow development in oil palm has not only been blamed on political instability for countries such as Nigeria and Liberia after they both went through civil wars, but also on low capital investments, land tenure systems and climatic factors to a lesser extent in other African countries.

This book describes the development of an economic cluster in Cameroon consequence of a knock-on-effect sparked off by the establishment of a hypothetical figure of 1 million hectares of oil palm plantation. It describes the socio economic advantages that come with such development. It also gives some light on how the crop can be grown sustainably and ways to mitigate conflicts in the sector.

Walter Ajambang

Cameroon, February 2018

Chapter 1 Oil Palm Production in Cameroon

The cultivation of oil palm is not new to Cameroon. Even before the establishment of the first industrial plantations, oil palm had been used as food especially by the coastal people of Cameroon. The Germans in Cameroon had identified an exceptionally thin-shelled palm fruit with high oil content as early as 1902. Agro industrial plantations were created by the Germans around the coastal regions bordering Mount Cameroon before the Second World War. The UNILEVER plantations and the Common Wealth Development Corporation also existed under British Southern Cameroons. In 1946, the Governor of British Cameroon signed an ordinance creating what is now known as the Cameroon Development Corporation (CDC). Other major foreign companies such as the Ferme Suisse, and national companies like PAMOL, CDC, SPOA, and SOCAPALM came to light before and immediately after the 1960 independence. After independence, all the major companies were public owned and functioned with public subventions and incentives for further especially for their extension programmes. The National Fund for Rural Development also known as FONADER was established and it operated between 1977 and 1991 to finance the expansion plantation agriculture such as the oil palm plantations with the aim of increasing production. The Cameroon Development Corporation created a special department to care for smallholders known as the Smallholders' Development Scheme while the SOCAPALM, SAFACAM and Ferme Swisse created the "Plantations Villageoise" or PV department. These structures supported smallholder farmers with inputs and technical support. In return, the smallholder farmers sold their Fresh Fruit Bunches FFB of oil palm to these Companies.

Nigeria was the world-leading exporter of palm oil before 1937 and between 1959 and 1970. West Cameroon contributed greatly to Nigeria's total palm oil production during this period because it was jointly administered with Nigeria. The two major companies of West Cameroon at the time; CDC and UNILEVER (PAMOL) exported their oil under Nigeria. For most of this period, Nigeria held centre stage as one of the largest producers and exporters of palm oil, accounting for more than 40% of global output in the 1950s (2% presently). At the time of the country's independence from British colonial rule in 1960, palm oil contributed 82% of Nigeria's national export revenue.

The early day oil palm companies did not place any importance on the protection of the environment because issues like global warming, Green House Gas concentration and other environmental hazards did not make headline news. Today, environmental issues have led to the concept of sustainable development and also concerns over the respect of indigenous rights. Companies are expected to achieve commercial success in ways that honour ethical values and respect people, communities, and the natural environment. Modern oil palm plantation practices provide for the establishment of plantations in respect of these issues. The oil palm industry besides practising sustainable development should also makes efforts to protect the rights of the indigenous people, wildlife and natural environment.

The Cameroonian rural population is very hard working and at least 3 out every 4 persons in rural areas are involved in farming. It is estimated that about 60% of the Cameroonian population earns life from farming and farming related activities. The CDC recruited the majority of its workers from the North West regions during its early days, the SOCAPALM and SAFACAM obtained labour from the Northern regions and part from the North West region as well. Today, all the regions of Cameroon supply labour to oil palm plantations. Annual production for Cameroon is 220 000 tons of oil and the industry is expecting an increase in cultivated land from current 300 000 hectares due to government support to famers and companies' extension programmes. Economic losses arising from the slow and negative growth of this industry and the increase in its local market price due to importation coupled with land shortages and environmental issues in South East Asia have created a favourable atmosphere for investors to come into Africa especially Cameroon and increase palm oil production. The challenges in achieving this will necessitate land reforms and the application of national and international regulations related to plantation development.

The geographical location of Cameroon provides suitability for oil palm cultivation in eight out of the ten regions of Cameroon. Oil palm can be grown from the Adamawa region towards the Southern parts of Cameroon.

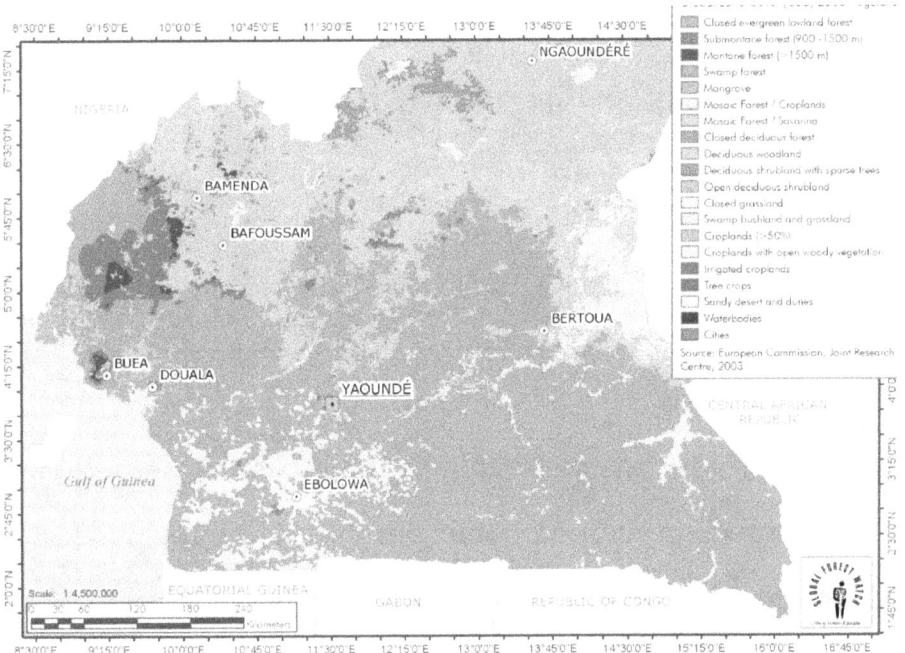

Fig. 1. Partial map of the Republic of Cameroon showing suitable areas for the cultivation of oil palm

We observe from the vegetation map of Cameroon that oil palm can be grown from the Southern part of Adamawa down to the border with the Republic of Gabon.

Table 1 shows the different suitability classes for the cultivation of oil palm. Oil palm grows well on the moderate and good classes. Most parts of Cameroon have between good and moderate climate suitability for oil palm cultivation.

Table 1. Climatic factors influencing oil palm cultivation

Characteristic	Suitability class			
	Good	Moderate	Severe	Very severe
Rainfall (mm)	25,00-	1,450-1,700	1,250-1,450	<1,250
Water deficit	0-150	150-250	250-400	>400
Dry season (mths)	None	1-2	2-4	>4
Solar radiation	13-15	9-11	7-9	<7
Mean temp (°C)	25-30	20-22	10-20	<16
Wind (m/s)	5-9	10-15	15-20	>20
pH	5-6	4.5-5	4-4.5 or 6.5-7	<4 or >7
Slope (%)	0-4	4-12	12-23	>30
Flooding	Never	Minor	Moderate	Severe
Drainage class	Good	Poor	Very	Very poor

The oil palm is a very tolerable crop with respect to agro climatic conditions. If production is for economic purpose, all production factors have to be optimized. Suitable oil palm land is found between Latitude 23.5° N and 23.5° S of the equator. This area includes Africa from the Gulf of Guinea through the Congo and East of Madagascar, Central and South America especially the Amazon, Columbia, Caribbean, South East Asia and the Pacific. Cameroon was estimated to have some 83 000 square kilometres of forest area suitable for the cultivation of oil palm in 2008. This area is situated in the eight most Southern Regions of Cameroon starting from the Adamawa Region. Production is best for oil palm if rainfall is ≥ 2000 mm/annum distributed the whole year with not more than 3 months of dry period (> 100 mm), 5 hours minimal daily sunshine and average temperature of 28°C.

Natural groves of oil palm were found in the North West and West regions of Cameroon. Some smallholder farmers have established oil palm plantations in these regions. There are some limiting factors that can greatly reduce the potential yield of oil palm in these regions. These include the low rainfall, low temperatures, high altitude and high slope gradient. The lowland and plains of the North West region can be used for plantation agriculture because they are moderately suitable. The South, South West and Littoral regions have good suitability for the cultivation of oil palm in industrial scale. The South West region is already crowded because it has been under plantation agricultural expansion for the past one hundred years. All the major industrial crops of Cameroon have large plantations in the South West region. A large part of the forest is under conservation as national parks. The other regions still have some land that can be exploited for oil palm plantation. The major factor limiting oil palm potential yield in Africa and especially Cameroon is the poor distribution of rainfall among the twelve months of the year.

Chapter 3 Multi-functionality of the palm oil

Ancient Africans saw palm oil as a source of food and medicine. Palm oil is also known as Crude Palm Oil (CPO), thus it can further be exploited and transformed into several valuable products. Palm oil is used in the manufacture of margarine, pharmaceuticals, soap and cosmetics, animal feed and organic manure, building material and furniture and bio fuel production. Oil palm production has favoured the development of upstream companies such as the seed industry, fertiliser, agrochemicals, agro mechanicals and financial services, side stream companies and downstream companies.

The Palm Kernel Oil (PKO) is also used to create a variety of value added products all of which we present in the following paragraphs.

1. The food industry

    - Refined and non refined cooking oil
    - Margarine, shortenings
    - Constituent ingredients in bread, biscuits and cake
    - Constituent ingredients in chocolate, milk and ice cream

Figure 2. The oil palm and its primary product

2. The pharmaceutical industry.

Oil palm has been used as a constituent ingredient in African traditional medicine. Its properties are being exploited today in modern medicine to provide drugs for certain diseases. Palm oil is a vegetable oil rich in vitamin A, D and E. Vitamin A in palm oil is so rich that it contains high levels of beta-carotene with values beyond 1.000 mg/kg depending on the origin of oil palm. The amount of pro vitamin A in palm oil has been estimated at 900 IU/g, which is higher than that obtained in fish oil (about 600 IU/g).

3. The cosmetic industry

    - Soap and detergents

    - Shampoo

    - Cream lotion

4. Dyes, candles, crayon industries

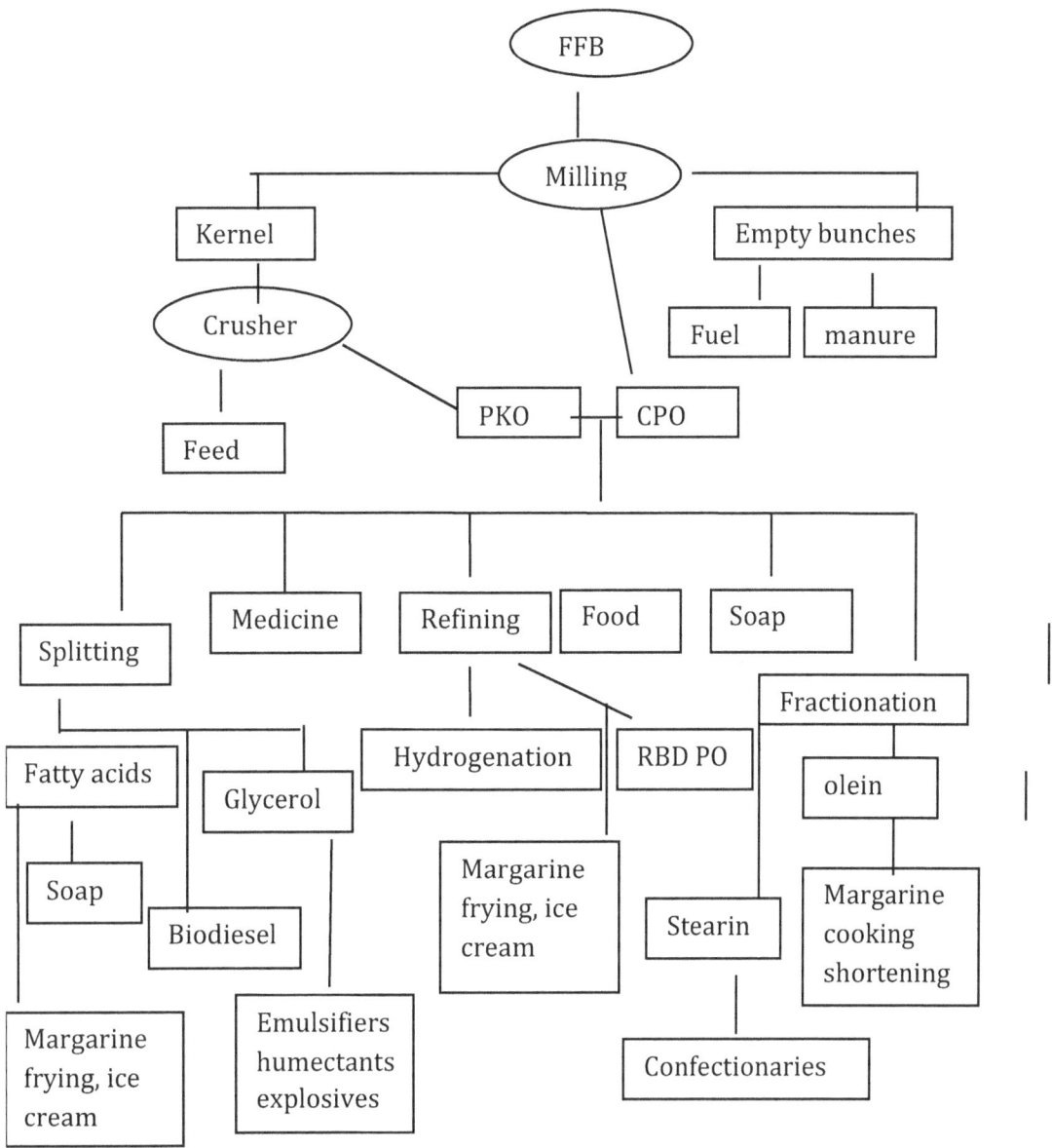

Fig. 3. Added value products from oil palm FFB

Chapter 4 The Oil Palm Industry: Fabrics of its Agribusiness

The oil palm industry is a huge industry due to its multiple products and rich value chain. The creation of oil palm plantations always pulls several other companies in both its upstream and downstream domains. Oil palm plantations create a hub for both public and private goods and services production. Below are some of the major ramifications of an oil palm agribusiness.

1. Upstream agribusiness

    - Agricultural tools and machines
    - Oil palm and cover crop seed industries
    - Fertilisers and other chemical industries
    - Housing and infrastructure

2. On-farm agribusiness

    - Smallholder plantations
    - Expansion of state owned plantations
    - Creation and expansion of foreign owned companies
    - Expansion and creation of council owned plantations

3. Downstream industries

    - Expansion of the soap industry
    - Expansion of the cosmetic industry
    - Expansion of the oleo-food industry
    - Creation of the bio diesel industry
    - Animal feed industry

4. Services

- Banks and other financial institutions
- Development of the stock market
- Insurances
- Land transport, seaports, airports, tours, hotels
- Shipping lines and airlines
- Environmental
- CPO and PKO trade
- Research and consultancies
- Vocational training institutions
- Certification institutions
- Quality control and quarantine
- Advocacies (Law firms)
- Environmental NGOs
- Labour unions

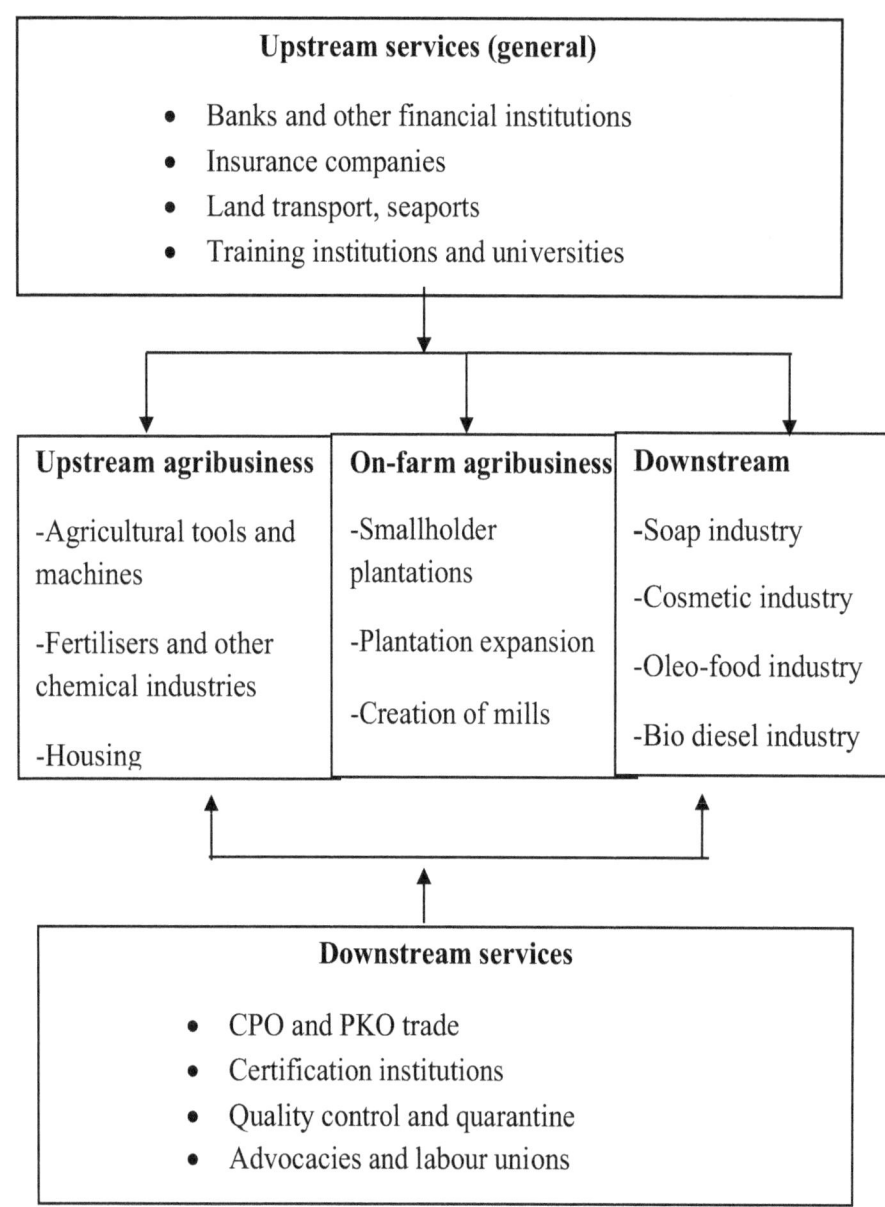

Upstream services (general)

- Banks and other financial institutions
- Insurance companies
- Land transport, seaports
- Training institutions and universities

Upstream agribusiness	**On-farm agribusiness**	**Downstream**
-Agricultural tools and machines	-Smallholder plantations	-Soap industry
-Fertilisers and other chemical industries	-Plantation expansion	-Cosmetic industry
-Housing	-Creation of mills	-Oleo-food industry
		-Bio diesel industry

Downstream services

- CPO and PKO trade
- Certification institutions
- Quality control and quarantine
- Advocacies and labour unions

Fig. 4. Scope of the oil palm industry in the national economy

Oil palm upstream Agribusiness

In 2007, one of the major oil palm companies in Cameroon was unable to plant its crop on time because of the late supply of seeds from the seed producing company. In 2011, a new oil palm company had to re adjust its schedule because the 3 million seeds they were expecting from a seed supplier in Cameroon were never delivered. They finally had to import seeds from South America and Asia in order to plant one year later. Upstream industries such as the seed, fertiliser and other inputs are strategically very important for the growth of plantation agriculture. The seed supplier in Cameroon could not supply such a huge quantity of seeds because its capacity was not built to support such large orders. With the expected increase in planted area, upstream industries such as the fertilisers, agricultural machines, seeds and other inputs shall commence to build their production capacity by the recruitment and training of man power, building of additional infrastructures, and getting more investment capital. The table below is an estimate of the number of related companies that may develop in Cameroon in order to support the establishment of oil palm plantations at the level of 1 million hectares.

Table 2. Development of upstream companies in Cameroon at the 1 million ha mark

Industry	Number of companies (SME)	Present situation
Agricultural tools and machines	10	1
Fertiliser and pesticides	25	3
Oil palm seed producers	5	2

Focusing on the seed industry alone, Cameroon shall need to develop the additional 700 000 hectares of oil palm with seeds from local companies. These companies shall be producing more than 140 million seeds for the establishment of new plantings. If we were to go by today's production statistics, it would take the 2 seed producers in Cameroon some 46 years to produce this quantity of seeds. Hence, it is imperative to increase the seed production capacity of CEREPAH La Dibamba and Pamol Lobe by at least 10 times each. The total planted area in Cameroon is estimated to undergo replanting at the rate of 4 % per year. This also needs seeds to be supplied by the same seed producers for these plantation regenerations alongside orders for the new plantings.

The establishment of an additional 700 000 ha of oil palm plantation shall also attract foreign companies such as those involved in heavy duty machines and farming tools. These companies may not only establish assembly plants but may also set up complete structures. There shall be a marked rise in the number of mechanical and electrical maintenance services for the engines that shall be used in the plantations. Most of the work done in the fertiliser companies in Cameroon at present consists of mixing the different components of fertilisers. With a huge market, companies shall see the need to build manufacturing structures and train personnel. Additional companies shall come in to complement the supplies. At this era of environmental friendly technologies, many organic manure producers shall either increase their capacity or may have to increase production units.

Fig. 5. Some upstream companies that may spring up as oil palm planting area increases in Cameroon

Downstream industries

These are post harvest related industries in the oil palm sector. They are involved in the processing of FFB to CPO, PKO and their derivatives. Factories shall be built to accommodate refining and fractioning departments. These factories shall produce frying oil, fatty acids and fatty alcohols, margarines, glycerines, shortenings and others. The following table gives an estimate of the number of downstream companies that would be developed following the production of 3.3 million tons of CPO.

Table 3. Downstream industries to be developed

Industry	Number of units	Present situation
CPO mills	30	07
Cooking oil refinery	06	02
Soap	100	12
Fatty alcohol	10	00
Margarine	4	02
Detergent	90	04
Bio diesel	02	00

Chapter 5 Importance to the economy

Oil palm is cultivated on approximately 15 million hectares across the world and consumption is expected to double by the year 2020. Oil palm (*Elaeis guineensis* Jacq.) is the world's leading oil crop with 37% of total world production of vegetable oil. Apart from its traditional use as a source of food, oil palm is used in the manufacture of margarine, pharmaceuticals, soap and cosmetics, animal feed and organic manure, building material and furniture and bio fuel production.

Oil palm is among the most productive and profitable of tropical crops for bio fuel production and production of biodiesel from oil palm has been increasing in recent years, particularly in Africa and Latin America.

Socio-economic benefits of a sustainable oil palm plantation could include poverty alleviation and long-term employment opportunities. Profit sharing may provide a further incentive, attracting more workers to the palm oil sector, along with better living and working conditions.

The rapid increase in plantation area in Malaysia, e.g. between 1970 and 1999 from 300 000 ha to 3.3 million ha, indicates the economic importance of this plantation crop and the growing world demand for palm oil. In Malaysia, the export value of crude palm oil and its derivatives rose from US$ 903 million of merchandise exports in 1980 (6.1% of the total) to US$ 13.8 billion in 2007. During the Asian financial crisis of 1997-1998, palm oil was Malaysia's most important source of foreign exchange. Likewise, Indonesia's palm oil export was behind the stabilisation of its economy during the 2008-2009 global economic crisis. The 10th Malaysia Plan, released in June 2010, aimed at increasing annual export earnings from palm oil by US$ $7.2 million to US$ 22.8 million. The palm oil industry is central to the success of the Malaysian economy and the livelihood of all Malaysians. The palm oil industry has been pivotal in building other Malaysian primary and secondary industries. From this base, the Malaysian economy could expand off from solid bedrock. Oil palm production has favoured the development of upstream companies such as the seed industry, fertiliser, agrochemicals, agro mechanicals and financial services, side stream companies and downstream companies.

Cameroon is yet to exploit 0.05% of its suitable land for the cultivation of oil palm, if we go by the statistics provided by   stickler et al in 2008. At present, Cameroon is yet to cover 400 000 ha of land for oil palm cultivation out of the total area of 8.3 million ha of its suitable land.

Increase in palm oil production

Considering that Cameroon shall soon meet the 1 million ha mark of oil palm plantations, some projections can be made from such a hypothetical figure. With 1 million ha of oil palm plantations, Cameroon shall produce about 3.3 million tons of CPO per year up from the barely 250 000 tons. Thus, Cameroon shall produce an additional 3 million tons of oil which shall fetch the Cameroonian economy some 1500 billions CFA if all the oil were to be consumed locally at 500 FCFA per kg. Considering that most of the new plantations currently being established in Cameroon are aiming at exporting their CPO, we estimate that more than 2 million tons of CPO shall be exported annually. This may fetch the country an average of 1400 million USD if the FOB price for CPO were to stand at 700 USD/ton. Total export for CPO and its related by-products and sub products may be estimated to fetch 21 million USD. It is worthy to note that the Cameroonian government recently obtained a 666 USD million loan deal from IMF to be disbursed in three yearly instalments. A developed oil palm industry alone would have produced this amount of money in the economy in a single year.

On an economic visit of the President of the Republic of Cameroon His Excellency Paul Biya told the Turkish business community that Cameroon has a potential market of more than 300 million people. He announced that this market includes the Central African Sub Region, the Federal Republic of Nigeria, the Democratic Republic of Congo and Sudan. And truly, this is a potential market for Cameroon's palm oil.

The palm oil industry has been pivotal in building other Malaysian primary and secondary industries. Below are a series of domains in which the palm oil industry can be used as the precursor of national development.

1. Employment: The CDC is often referred as the second employer after the state of Cameroon. The CDC is an agro – industry that directly employs tens of thousands of Cameroonian family heads. A number of small businesses in Cameroon and especially in the South West Region are solely dependent on the CDC. The oil

palm industry in Cameroon alone employs more than 20 000 workers both directly and indirectly. The same industry employs more than 7 million workers in Indonesia. Therefore, the Palm oil industry is a source for jobs. With 1 million ha under oil palm cultivation, Cameroon can add more than 100,000 direct and indirect jobs.

2. Infrastructure: Citing the director of the Environmental Conservation Department of the State of Sabah in Malaysia, I quote

"Oil palm cultivation is one of the main economic activities of the state, which not only effects extensive land development but also provides substantial revenue to the state as well as the nation as a whole. It is also one of the pivotal aspects that act as the catalyst for regional infrastructural development, particularly road network within interior areas".

It is worth recalling that the Tiko port was created to ship fresh agricultural produce such as banana, pepper and rubber. The development of plantations would need that goods are transported at the nearest ports because of their perishable nature. This shall give way to the creation of new ports and the increase in traffic of old ports. Rivers such as the Mungo and Meme, including the Manyu may become very instrumental in the transportation of agricultural products. The Wharfs Idenau, Ekondo Titi and Mundemba may experience an increase in traffic. It is no secret that logging companies created most of our rural roads. The bitter truth is that when there is no production in any certain area, no body including the government and other international funding bodies shall accept to build a road in such a location. The existing plantation companies in Cameroon have also contributed a lot to the construction of roads which in most areas are also serving villages close to these plantations. There is a possibility that one of the airports of Tiko or Mamfe becomes operational again. International scientists and consultants who would be called to come and investigate certain problems in the plantations are mostly paid by hours and most of them have limited time. Expatriates working in the companies may not like to live around the estates and would like to fly-in every morning or every Monday morning. Other movements would create the necessary traffic for the functioning of our local airports. This situation has happened elsewhere and Cameroon will not be an exception.

In this modern context when Corporate Social Responsibility (CSR) is becoming the winning business model especially in natural resource sectors, most of the villages shall be supplied with electricity from their neighbouring plantations. The supply of water to nearby villages and the building of schools had been done by agro-industrial companies. Cameroonian agro-industries companies provided electricity at the time they were under state ownership. After privatization of some of these companies, they focused on the capitalistic principle of profit maximization, without too much attention to villagers' needs. With the advent of democracy and that of indigenous people rights, plantation owners have discovered that the only means of producing sustainably is by assisting the nearby villages in their socio-economic endeavours. The concept of Corporate Social Responsibility (CSR) that in many countries has already moved from voluntary to regulatory, has given the opportunity to villagers to benefit from the occupation of their lands by agro industries.

New companies that shall establish in areas such as the Nkam Division, Kupe Mwanenguba Division and Manyu divisions shall have the tasks to transform these places to look like the Fako division with a dense road network both rural and paved. This may become reality in a time space of less than 15 years after company's implantation. The concept of CSR makes sure that companies create schools and hospitals in which they can treat company workers and villagers alike. Markets shall be created in locations that are central to all other villages. The development of the Muea market in Buea Sub Division was due to the major agro industrial company based in Fako Division. Workers attended this market on Sundays from all the plantation estates to procure basic food and other household needs. It was always full to capacity on planation pay out because special transportation was made available by company's authorities to workers for shopping. This special occasion was known as "enjoyment". Today, the Muea market stands as one of the biggest food markets in the Central African Sub Region supplying food to Gabon, Equatorial Guinea and Central African Republic. The area known as Nguti in the Kupe Mwanenguba is a business hub in making. The location of this village makes it possible for it to play the role of a "Muea Market" or a "Douala" in the next coming decade with the eminent creation of agro industries in this area.

Rural development arising from the establishment of a neighbouring agro industry is very evident in countries where CSR is regulated by law. Countries such as Indonesia that has large expanses of uninhabited forests with isolated villages in distant islands could not have developed if everything was left in the hands of government alone. Roads linking provinces in the massive Borneo island of Indonesia and Malaysia came to existence only after oil palm companies were established in these areas. Natural resource economists have done so much research and all of them come to the conclusion that the establishment of oil palm plantations in these areas has been a major catalyst in the development of these areas.

Also worthy to recall is the fact that the government knew very well that development in the rural areas would only be spear headed by agriculture and that is why in the early days after independence they created many agricultural development projects in rural areas. These "Societes de Developppement" had more social objectives than profit maximisation motives. In areas such as the Nkam, the government had developed projects known as trans migration in which agriculture was the main occupation of the new inhabitants. In areas where these projects failed, development also been slow if not stagnant.

The relationship between oil palm industry and other sectors of the economy

1. Linkage effects

The impact of oil palm industry on the whole national economy can be analysed using several mechanisms. The *forward linkage effect ratio* and the *backward linkage effect* are some of the indices used to analyse the role of a sector in a global economy.

The backward linkage effect index calculates the impact created by a change in output of the palm oil industry to the output of other economic sectors in the country as a result of using inputs from other sectors. The forward linkage effect studies the impact to the whole national economy created by the use of output from the palm oil industry as input to the other sectors of the economy. In a relatively similar economy like ours, studies carried out have shown that the oil palm on-farm agribusiness has a forward linkage effect of 2.36. This ratio implies that if palm oil production increases by 1 million CFA, it will spark off an increase of 2.36 million CFA in the whole economy. Hence, an increase of total cultivated area of 1 million hectares shall push national evenue by 2.36 X 1500 billions (or 3540 billions CFA). Other aspects of the oil palm agribusiness such as the downstream and upstream sectors have also shown higher indices. In simple terms, the oil palm industry shall push the development of all other economic sectors related to its growth. This includes industries concerned with inputs and industries that shall use palm oil products as their own inputs. The more the hectarage, the more the increase in national economy, especially those aspects linked to the services and products of oil palm. Related sectors such as banks, insurance, advocacies, NGOs, consultancies, manufacturing industries and many others shall experience expansion. Expansion in this case means increase in production, profit and the amount of labour employed. This indicates that the creation of oil palm plantations in the Southern part of Cameroon shall boost the economy of Cameroon especially that of the regions concerned.

2. Multiplier effects

We can also estimate the impact of an oil palm plantation business on the national economy by looking at the various multiplier effects associated to the business. These multiplier effects in the economy include the output multiplier effect, the income multiplier effect, the employment multiplier effect and the value added multiplier effect.

So much research has been carried out in this domain and it has been revealed that the oil palm agribusiness can yield and output multiplier effect of more than 1.71 in its on-farm agribusiness and also more than 2.04 in its downstream sector.

Trade Balance

Today, Cameroon cannot compete with China or other Asian nations in the domain of electronics and ICTs. There are no production industriues for computers, cell phones and other minor electrical appliances in Cameroon. Cameroon is therefore doomed to import all of these as of now. However, Cameroon has a comparative advantage on some of the major agricultural products that can enable it push export revenue and reverse balance deficit. Consider that Cemeroonian palm oil production deficit gap stands at 130 000 tons of oil annually (Association of producers, CT 04/07/2017). It would imply that Cameroon has to spend a total of 700 X 130 000 USD or 91 000 000 USD or 50 billion CFA (50 000 000 000 FCFA). The development of the oil palm agro industry alone can reverse Cameroon's negative trade balance in the space of 10 years which stood at about 694 billions in 2015. This reverse can take 2 years because Cameroon is a potential exporter of palm oil.

Chapter 6 Environmental Fears

Several worries arise concerning the use of vast areas of land for the cultivation of oil palm. These issues concern claims such as the overexploiting and merciless destruction of rainforests, the genocide of forests' most charismatic and magnificent animals such as the Gorillas, the Chimpanzees, Orangutans and other endangered wild life. Some other claims give concerns over the cultivation of oil palm on peat soils and the use of unsustainable farm practices such as bush burning. There are also reservations about soil conservation practices in oil palm plantations that may lead to erosion, mudflow and landslides. Others point to the excessive use of chemicals and their impacts on both humans and animals. Fears also arise from the amount of atmospheric pollution caused by the milling of CPO and effluent discharge.

Oil palm plantations are net absorbers of one of the major green house gases; CO_2. The process of photosynthesis in green plants leads to the uptake of CO_2 during carbohydrate production and the release of CO_2 during energy use. The difference between these two processes gives us the net carbon dioxide production by plants and in this case, Oil palm is a net absorber of CO_2. According to research results, an oil palm plantation absorbs 64.5 tons of CO2/ha/year while the net CO_2 absorption for a tropical rainforest is lower (42.4 tons CO_2/ha/year). The role of oil palm planation as a net absorber of CO_2 should be a motivation for investors and policy makers to promote the cultivation of the oil palm that is also the highest productive oil crop per surface area. Besides the absorption of CO_2, the oil palm also releases net oxygen (O_2) into the air during the same processes of photosynthesis and respiration. The oil palm plantation plays a major role in the water cycle in the ecosystem. The processes of evapo-transpiration and photosynthesis assures the take up of soil water by the roots, through the trunk and then part of it is released in the leaves as vapour. Oil palm plantations shall always conserve water and soil especially when best management practices BMP are enforced. The extensive canopy cover and the cover crop planted under the trees reduce soil water loss and soil erosion through leaching and surface run-offs. Oil palm has been cultivated on the hillsides along the road from Mutengene to Limbe since 1964. The cultivation of oil palm on these relatively high gradient slopes has avoided landslides and mudflow on these relatively sloped areas. On the other side of the same hill, landslides and mudflow takes place every rainy season with the loss of lives and property in quarters like Towe and West-end New Town Limbe. A heavy landslide took place in New Town around 2002 in which 9 people lost their lives due to mudflow and landslide caused by other anthropogenic uses of forests. Oil palm can contribute to the conservation of nature if good agricultural practices (GAP) are employed while respecting all national and international regulations associated with its cultivation.

Fig. 6. Oil palm cultivated on the slopes of hills near between Mutengene and Limbe highway since 1964

National and international regulations have paved the way for farmers to be able to produce crops without depleting the environment. These regulations are based upon modern and endogenous technologies which lead to higher crop production with low chemical in puts. Cameroon also has a National Biodiversity Strategic Action Plan (NSBAP), which outlines the criteria for using all the different ecosystems in Cameroon for socio-economic purposes. These regulations, if adequately enforced by governments, shall go a long way to mitigate global warming and climate change. The objective of the state of Cameroon is to have 30% of its national territory declared as protected area; at the moment the number stands at a little over 15%. The Kyoto Protocol of 1998 defined strategies to mitigate green house gases GHG and elaborated the Clean Development Mechanism (CDM) on emission limitation and reduction.

In its Article 2, the Kyoto Protocol took the engagement to reduce their overall GHG emissions by at least 5 per cent below 1990 levels in the commitment period 2008 to 2012. Also, in its Article 10, the Protocol states that there shall be cooperation in the promotion of effective modalities for the development, application and diffusion of, and take all practicable steps to promote, facilitate and finance, as appropriate, the transfer of, or access to, environmentally sound technologies, know-how, practices and processes pertinent to climate change, in particular to developing countries, to promote and enhance the transfer of, and access to, environmentally sound technologies.

Article 12 of the Kyoto Protocol states that developing countries shall benefit from project activities resulting in certified emission reductions and that CDM shall assist in arranging funding of certified project activities as necessary.

Researchers are working day and night to come up with measures that shall boost production in a sustainable manner. It is a great challenge to any agricultural firm today if its products are not labelled as 'sustainable'. The oil palm industry has a "Watch Dog" known as the Roundtable on Sustainable Palm Oil RSPO that defines the criteria for the production of palm oil in the world. The RSPO which is assisted by national and international NGOs defines the criteria from land acquisition to palm oil delivery. It has regulated all the elements of the oil palm value chain and it would be interesting to keep watch on companies so that oil palm development can be sustainable.

How can Cameroon attain palm oil sufficiency without deforestation

It will be an uphill task for any investor to obtain land concessions ammounting to tens of thousand hectares in Cameroon. International and national pressure would not permit the government to give such concessions for oil palm cultivation. It is easy for Cameroon to avoid confrontations with NGOs related to palm oil production. Since Cameroon is in deficit of production, it can develop strategies to attain palm oil self-sufficiency without further deforestation.

1. Cameroon government should improve on the investement and management of its two lame agro-industries; the CDC and PAMOL. The Ministry of economy can give credits to these companies to modernise their production systems including the building of mills.

2. Improve productivity of existing smallholder farmers such that national palm oil production should reflect total hectarage under smallholdings.

3. Fund and support smallholder farmers through agro-industries such as PAMOL, CDC, SOCAPALM. Money should be placed at the disposal of these companies, which in turn shall implement programmes to develop and improve upon the productivity of smallholder plantations. Funding of smallholder farmers through government agencies such as Projet de Developpement des Palmaraies Villageoise (PDPV) and Projet de Developpement des Chaines de Valeurs Agricoles (PDCVA) shall continue to yield the results that they are currently yielding.

Chapter 7 Health worries

On the 15th of November 2012, the French Senate approved the Nutella amendment that would quadruple tax on palm oil, which is a key ingredient in the chocolate spread in order to discourage the consumption of the oil. They said that palm oil is rich in saturated fats and their harmful effect on health has been established. Major palm oil producers such as Malaysia and Indonesia reacted immediately calling the move unfounded and irresponsible, noting that people get most of their fats from eating meat and cheese.

Though palm oil contains almost equal proportions of saturated and unsaturated fatty acids, palmitic acids may only have an undesirable effect if the amount of linoleic acid in the diet is low. Some benefits of palm oil to human health include;

Anti oxidants effects: the tocopherols and tocotrienols in palm oil provide the human body with anti oxidants which are capable of scavenging free radicals and reactive oxygen species (ROS) thereby protecting human cells against oxidative damage. Human cell oxidation leads to early ageing, cancer and inflammatory diseases.

Inhibition of cholesterol synthesis: the gamma and delta isomers of tocotrienols are capable of lowering and inhibiting cholesterol synthesis at the liver. Supplementary consumption of tocotrienol-enriched palm oil results in a significant reduction of serum cholesterol.

Chapter 8 Social Fears

A report by the High Level Panel of Experts on Food Security and Nutrition (HLPE) asserts that between 50 and 80 million hectares of land, most of which is in low income countries have been subject to negotiations by international investors in the last five years. Local people are *particularly vulnerable if their lands and resources are transformed, encroached upon by outsiders, or significantly degraded. Their languages, cultures, religions, spiritual beliefs, and institutions may also be under threat. As a consequence, Indigenous Peoples may be exposed to different types of risks, and the impacts associated with project development may be more severe than on non-indigenous communities. This may include loss of identity, culture, and natural resource-based livelihoods, as well as exposure to impoverishment and diseases*

National and international protocols including regulations have been set concerning the acquisition and management of land for industrial or plantation development. It would be appropriate for companies not only to abide to these conventions but also to be in good terms with the local communities in order to successfully carry out their activities.

Most oil palm producing nations are becoming more democratic in their form of governance. This gives an opportunity for local and indigenous people to claim their rights over natural resources including land. At first, land was attributed to companies in an arbitrary manner with no prior consent sought from the villagers. This was nevertheless a time bomb because indigenous people have started to fight back in this era of liberalisation and freedom. They have been using various approaches such as rioting on companies' plantation site, destruction of companies' property and plantation, killing of companies' staff and also through legal channels. Many companies that had developed plantations in those early days have started abandoning them in the face of such problems.

Fruit theft has been a major social issue hampering oil palm production in Cameroon. The problem of low production and productivity as a result of palm fruit theft, oil palm plantation reconversion to less vulnerable crops and the abandon of whole plantations could have been avoided if for the past 40 years, oil palm companies had implemented programmes which could lead to socio economic development of its neighbouring villages. These programmes would have included;

1. There should be a Free, Prior and Informed Consent FPIC of the villagers and indigenes before any land is exploited for industrial use. This should be a strong commitment between the government, the local people and the company. Communities should be associated in all the levels of negotiation

2. The reservation of farmland to indigenes or neighbouring villages so that they could cultivate crops not only for subsistence but also for the local market. This could help pay school fees for their children.

3. The creation and financing of schools including the award of scholarships to local youths and their eminent employment into the company. This aspect is very important today in every

business operation especially those operating in less developed economies. There is a sense of ownership that develops in families whose relatives work in these companies. Family members of employees seek to preserve the well being of the company rather than being frustrated because none of the kin men holds a staff position in the company. Another reason is that employees tend to educate their children, and close relatives from their salaries as workers to these companies. Those relatives who have been educated shall in turn obtain jobs rather than stay uneducated and unemployed in the villages with the sole hope to become a fruit theft.

4. The establishment and subsequent continuous technical support to smallholder farmers in order to build up their economic capacity and help to absorb labour that could not be employed by the big companies. Most smallholder farms have been abandoned because of the absence of technical support, unavailability of farm inputs and the use of poor planting materials.

It is believed that if indigenes and the local surrounding populations are involved in the process leading to the establishment of companies on their land, companies will develop in a peaceful and stable environment, which is a key factor for their productivity. If companies put in place strategies that will help in the development of local communities, then they will become economically viable and will not depend on the companies' assets for survival. Those companies, which at the beginning of their establishment, proceed to supplying social amenities such as hospitals, roads, schools and the award of scholarships to students in the local communities, shall reap the benefits of these investments indirectly on their productivity through an enabling environment. The countries with the highest production of oil palm developed several strategies to mitigate the economic burden of local natives and surrounding community on their plantations. By this policy, investors were asked to create plantations with at least 20% ownership in the hands of indigenes. The 20% comprising of between 2-4 hectares per farmer would surround the remaining 80% also known as the nucleus. In a set up like this one, the local people have a stable economic activity and the company's plantation would be secured from fruit theft. In these countries, Government Central Bank awarded low rate loans to community agencies in order to develop smallholder plantations. Other community services included technical support to smallholder farmers from seed supply, road construction and maintenance, plantation upkeep, fertiliser and herbicide supply recommendation on harvesting, transport facilities and milling of their FFB.

Apart from actively involving the local population, companies also develop social amenities for the local community such as the construction and maintenance of roads, the building of markets, supply of electricity, supply of pipe borne water and the construction of schools. Companies also give bursaries to outstanding students of the community to specialise in one of the fields in agriculture and so that he can earn a place in the company upon graduation.

Social benefits from some oil palm companies to local communities

Recently the world's biggest oil palm company from Malaysia offered scholarships for Liberians students into Malaysian top universities and also into Liberian universities. The recent initiative was praised by Liberian President, Ellen Johnson Sirleaf, who commented that: "Education has been a challenge in the past for our young people and Sime Darby's effort to support education is very good."

The Liberian President recently concluded a business deal with the second biggest oil palm company SINARMAS Agribusiness and Food, an Indonesian based Limited Liability Company awarding them some 220 000 hectares of land to develop oil palm. SINARMAS is currently training Liberians to work in the plantations that are being created. This initiative will create tens of thousands of jobs in the post-war Liberia.

Are companies created with the sole goal of profit maximisation?

From its etymology, a company comes from the Latin word *'cum* and *'panis'* which means breaking the bread together. This might have inspired Dave Packard, the founder of Hewlett Packard Company concerning the goal of establishing a company. He said and I quote " *I think many people assume, wrongly, that a company exist simply to make money. While this is an important result of a company's existence, we have to go deeper and find the real reasons for our being.*

As we investigate this, we inevitably come to the conclusion that a group of people get together and exist as an institution that we call a company so that they are able to accomplish something that they could not achieve separately, they make contribution to the society, a phrase which sounds trite but is fundamental". Companies bring wealth to the national economy but may cause negative environmental and social impacts on its surrounding environment and society. The concept of Corporate Social Responsibility (CSR) therefore finds its rationale. A country like Indonesia has included CSR activities in their laws on companies. Some of these laws include; (a) Law No. 23 of 1997 concerning the protection of the environment in its article 6(1), 6(2), 16(1) and 17(1). (b) Law No. 40 of 2007 concerning the Social and Environmental Responsibility. This law is a commitment for companies to contribute to the sustainable development of the national economy while improving the quality of life and environment of its workers, the local surrounding communities and to the whole nation. In its article 74, the law No. 40 of 2007 stipulates that Social and Environmental Responsibility is an obligation to all companies operating in the field of natural resources. CRS activities for companies like Sampoerna Agro, PT Smart and PT ASTRA Agro of Indonesia include Education (Building schools, training teachers, scholarships, study loans,) Health and wealth creation. Until CSR is set as an obligation on companies exploiting rural environments, the rural populations surrounding the agro industries shall continue to live in depravation, poverty and illiteracy. The absence of socio economic amenities and high unemployment in the surrounding villages has led to villagers depending on FFB theft for their livelihoods. The non existence of assistance (supply of improved/high yielding seed varieties, fertilizer, technical advice, crop evacuation and processing) to surrounding oil palm smallholder farmers and poor economic situation of neighbouring communities, might have contributed to the dependency on oil palm fruit theft from companies' plantations as a source of living by the youths in these surrounding villages.

Herakles Farms put its CSR program in public and below is a summary. Herakles Farms could not grow because of excessive NGO pressure on both Cameroonian government and Herakles management. In a country like Indonesia or Malaysia, Herakles Farms would have thrived because these countries have the resources to fight back pressure from International NGOs and International Financial institutions.

CSR program presented by Herakles Farms to the public on October 22, 2012

Herakles Farms, an American agriculture company focused on identifying and implementing solutions to important food security issues in Africa, today announced that it has awarded college scholarships to 26 Cameroonian students in a newly established merit-based program that recognizes the academic achievement of some of the nation's most promising undergraduates.

The scholarship fund is just one initiative within Herakles Farms' larger community development program that is designed to support the economic prosperity and growth of Cameroon, where it is developing a sustainable palm oil project. The scholarship fund is named in honor of the late Dr. Isidore Timti , who served as Herakles Farms' Country Director, and will provide unprecedented educational opportunities for students so that they may overcome the financial barriers that would otherwise hold them back from pursuing advanced education and career goals. Dr. Timti was a long-time champion of local capacity building, skills training and job creation, which are areas of priority that Herakles Farms integrates into every stage of its planning and development. During summer breaks and have the opportunity to join Herakles Farms as a full-time employee upon successful completion of their studies and internships.

"Herakles Farms is deeply committed to expanding our support for the people of Cameroon – especially those who reside near our palm oil project – not only through job creation, but also through our community development programs," said Bruce Wrobel , CEO of Herakles Farms. "The Dr. Isidore Timti Memorial Scholarship Fund will help the next generation of students become world-class leaders in the global economy.

Areas of study eligible for the scholarship include: crop science; agronomy; engineering; forestry; environmental science; accounting, finance, marketing and business management; and nursing.

Herakles Farms donated food to 1,700 households in 38 villages located in the Nguti subdivision of Kupe-Muanenguba and in Mundemba and Toko in Ndian. In total, 11 tons of rice and 10 tons of fish were distributed to more than 8,000 individuals in the Nguti, Mundemba and Toko areas.

In addition to the food program, Herakles Farms has been providing the St. John of God Hospital Nguti with electricity between the hours of 6:00 p.m. and 6:30 a.m. Through Herakles Farms' support, the hospital has been able to improve its services and save lives by attending to emergency cases, performing deliveries and other services at night that require a constant flow of electricity. The hospital has also been able to reduce operating costs associated with running a generator throughout the night.

Chapter 9 Economic contribution of Cameroon's natural oil palm to the development of the global oil palm industry

Cameroon is situated in West-Central Africa at the Atlantic coast (Gulf of Guinea) sharing borders with Central African Republic, Chad, Congo, Equatorial Guinea, Gabon and Nigeria. The southern part of Cameroon is embedded in the second mega bio-diversity in the world; The Congo basin. It has a total area of 475,440 km^2 and having a mosaic of vegetation and landscape that has earned it the name "Africa in Miniature". The Cameroon's oil palm wild material is believed to contain some interesting genotypes, given its agro climatic diversity and long standing history of wild genotype provider to many genebanks in the world. Cameroon has served as a major provider for genetic material in the world palm oil industry. Wild oil palm genotypes have been collected from the forests and hinterlands of Cameroon and taken across the continents of the world to develop and produce the best high yielding oil palm varieties. Many oil palm collection expeditions have been recorded in Cameroonian oil palm history. Table 1 summaries some of the major expeditions where Cameroon wild oil palm accessions were collected from its natural groves and taken to the best oil palm research centres in the world.

Table 4. Summary of expeditions carried out in Cameroon's natural oil palm grove destined to breed high improved varieties

Year	Collectors	Location	Destination

1848	Dutch explorers	Gulf of Guinea	Indonesia
1967	Blaak (Dutch)	Ekona, Widikum	Indonesia and Malaysia
1974 1975	Institut de Recherches sur les Huiles et Oleagineueses (IRHO) - France	Muyuka, Mamfe, Kendem, Kumba, Widikum	French African Countries
1984	Unilever and Palm Oil Research Institute of Malaysia (PORIM)	West and East Cameroon	Malaysia
1996	Blaak and Sterling	Bamenda highlands	Costa Rica and Asia
2007	CENIPALMA	7 southern regions of Cameroon	Columbia
2008	Indonesian Palm Oil Board (IPOB)	7 Southern regions of Cameroon	Indonesia, Malaysia

Blaak (1976) collected material from the Widikum and Ekona regions of Cameroon in 1967 of which have been widely used to develop the majority of oil palm planting seed today. In another of his collection expeditions in Cameroon, Blaak and Sterling (1996) found out that some oil palms were able to produce satisfactorily between 1000 to 2000 m above sea level. Twenty years of breeding using DAMI deli crossed with Cameroon and Tanzanian selections of African oil palm have led to the development of precocious bearing, cold tolerant oil palms (Chapman *et al.* 2003). It is in this light that the Indonesian Oil Palm Board DMSI carried out an exploration of wild oil palm genotypes in Cameroon in 2008.

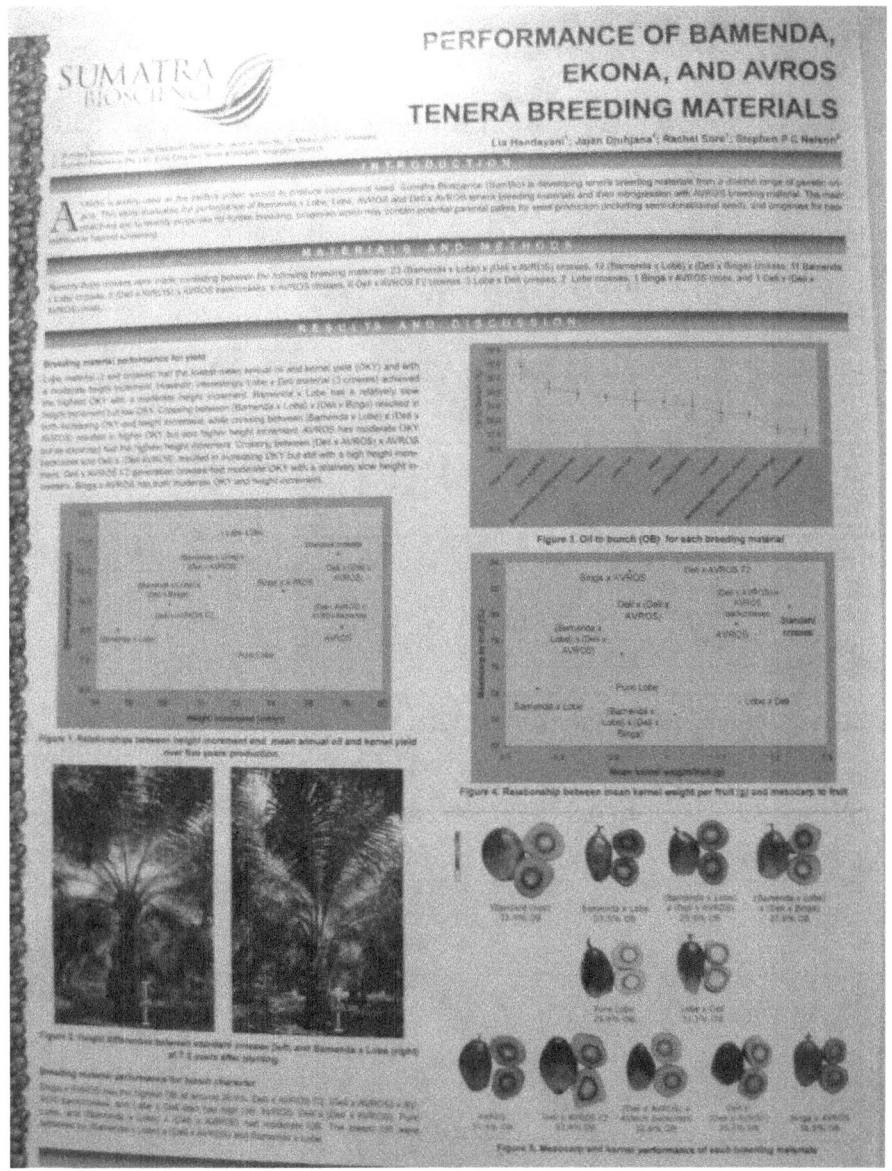

Figure 7. Presentation on the performance of oil palm genetic material collected from Cameroon in an international conference in The Westin Resort International Bali Island, Indonesia 2010

Annual income generated from the sales of planting material from Cameroonian origin can be estimated at 10 750 000 000 for Indonesia alone. In the same line, income generated from the sale of Crude Palm oil CPO obtained from Cameroon planting material could be estimated as 2000 billion F cfa.

Table 5. Oil palm varieties that are produced from seeds originating from Cameroon

Company	Country	Cross
PT London Sumatra	Indonesia	Dura Deli X Pisifera **Ekona BL**
PT Tunggal Yunus	Indonesia	Dura Deli X Pisifera **Ekona 21**
PT Sampoerna Agro	Indonesia	Dura Deli X Pisifera **Ekona BSM**
PT Tania Selatan	Indonesia	Deli Dura X Pisifera **Ekona TS**
Sumatra Bioscience	Indonesia	**Pure Lobe**
Sumatra Bioscience	Indonesia	**Bamenda X Lobe**
Sumatra Bioscience	Indonesia	**(Bamenda X Lobe) X** (Deli X Binga)
Sumatra Bioscience	Indonesia	**Bamenda X** Avros) X (Deli X Avros)
Sumatra Bioscience	Indonesia	**Lobe X** Deli

ASD Costa Rica	Costa Rica	**Bamenda** X AVROS
ASD Costa Rica	Costa Rica	**Bamenda** X **Ekona**
ASD Costa Rica	Costa Rica	Tanzania X **Ekona**

Source: Ditjenbun 2010. Directorate General of Estate Crops Indonesia. The names in bold indicate parents material from Cameroon.

The figure below shows two oil palm varieties developed by Indonesian Research Institutes from wild material obtained in Cameroon. It took many years of breeding efforts to obtain the final variety shown in the picture. The varieties are named according to the origin of the principal parent breeding materials that are from Ekona and Bamenda in Cameroon.

Figure 8. Oil palm varieties developed through genetic improvement from Cameroon wild accessions in an exhibition in Jakarta Conventional Centre, Indonesia 2009.

The varieties originating from Cameroon have several outstanding and desirable traits. The Ekona varieties have a high Oil Extraction Rate (OER) and they are high yielding (7 tons FFB/ha/yr). The Bamenda varieties have moderate height increment per year, they are cold tolerant and can grow on high altitudes.

The overall contribution of Cameroon's material to global palm oil industry can be summarised in the following points;

- FFB yields were between 22 and 30 t/ha/yr while OTB ratio ranged between 23.77% and 31.2% by the end of the second cycle

- Disease resistant varieties, slow growth, high nutritional value, pro-healthy, ecologically adapted, climate change tolerant,

- The Ekona Cw6 2/2311 variety has high yields, high oil extraction rates, low incidence of crown diseases and high number of bunches.

- Global production rose from < 1 million to 45 million tons/year.

- >11 billion francs CFA from seed sales.

- >2000 billions CFA from palm oil sales (Cameroon 2016 budget ~ 4000 billions CFA)

- **Agro-climatic factors**

  a. **Land**: According to Sticker et al. 2008, Cameroon has 83,000 km² of suitable land for oil palm cultivation while Malaysia with similar population has 146,000 km². Indonesia has 617, 000 km² on which most of its 240 million population is not evenly distributed. The vast forests of Borneo and Papua are highly under populated with less than 10% of the total population. Land might not be a limiting factor because as earlier stated the Cameroon government's goal is to protect at least 30% of its land.

  b. **Rainfall**: The amount of annual rainfall is high and suitable for oil palm production. The limiting factor is that there is a distinct dry season in Cameroon with several months not recording a single drop of land. The uneven distribution of rainfall among the twelve months of the year is the main cause for fall in production in most sub-Saharan countries. There is a water deficit that has negative impacts on both growth and production of oil palm. Therefore, oil palm will tend to produce more sterile male flowers during the dry season.

  c. **Investment banks**. In a country like Indonesia, there is a Ministry of cooperatives, while in Malaysia, there is a Ministry of plantations Development. These ministries are actively involved in the financing and development of smallholder plantations. There are other government-specialised programs that provide financial assistance and low rate loans to smallholder farmers. There is an active stock exchange market in these countries; Bursa Efek Indonesia (BEI) in which most oil palm companies can raise investment capital. In Malaysia, more than 43 oil palm companies are listed in the Bursa Malaysia KLSE, which has a market capitalisation of 35.4 billion USD or 21,240 billion CFA. Locally, companies and individuals in Malaysia and Indonesia can generate investment capital internally and from local banks to create plantations. Unlike in Africa where most companies coming into Africa have to pass through the World Bank (WB) and International Financial Corporation (IFC) in order to raise capital for plantation establishment. The WB and IFC are very sensitive to environmental issues and it is easier for any funding to be blocked by these institutions because of environmental complaints from international NGOs.

d. **Economies of scale**: The basic tools, equipment and to some extent skilled labour are not close to companies in Cameroon. Most it is imported from Europe, America and Asia. It will take many weeks to months to import and replace a spare part in an oil mill in Cameroon. Within this time, production will either stop or slow down. Cost of production will increase because FFB has to be sent to distant oil mills. In Malaysia and Indonesia, all supporting industries are at arms length. The seed industry, the agrochemicals, the farm equipment industry and others.

e. **Competitiveness**: Companies in South East Asia are highly competitive because of the ease with which they can obtain finances, equipment and cheap labour. The cost of production of a ton of CPO in South East Asia is USD 320 as against USD 500 for Cameroon. It would therefore be difficult to find external markets when compared to South East Asian countries.

f. **Technical aspects**: There are famous agricultural universities in Malaysia and Indonesia. There are other specialised institutions that train skilled labour on specific crops or plantation crop production. There are high technology laboratories and renowned research centres involved in crop development and socio-economic studies.

g. **NGO pressure**: Indonesia and Malaysia have the resources to withstand NGO pressure. Although these resources are not lacking in African countries, they however need to be developed.

h. **Markets**: The biggest markets are found in Asia. Indonesia alone is more than 250 million inhabitants. They have cultural links with countries like China and India, which are the two biggest markets in the world. African countries are too fragmented with complicated borders. Moreover, European markets are very exigent in quality.

Chapter 11: Sustainable oil palm production

When the world politicians, civil servants and experts met to discuss "Our Common Future" in 1987 they suggested that growth and environmental maintenance are not mutually exclusive. In what became known as the "Brundtland" report, they defined sustainable development as "...development that meets the needs of the present without compromising the ability of future generations to meet their own needs". A few years later, the delegates to the 1992 Earth Summit in Rio de Janeiro refined this definition by linking economic growth (profit), environmental protection (planet) and social equity (people) in a blue print for sustainability in the 21st. century.

Sustainable agriculture must be based on the following three pillars; People, Planet and Profit. Firstly, of protecting the society i.e. the people with food quality and safety, improving farmers' skills and raising rural social and economic conditions; secondly, of protecting the environment i.e. the planet with optimum use of natural resources and minimum input requirements on soil, water, air, energy and maintenance of a large number of varieties and species according to local conditions and preserving and improving wildlife habitats; and thirdly improving the economy i.e. profit where the challenge is to provide food for a growing population at an affordable prices. Where there is good input/output efficiency, application of modern technologies, and optimising utilization of products, minimizing losses and enhancing positive economic benefits. The oil palm is a perennial crop which stays green all round the year. It is estimated that the oil palm uses about 64 tons of CO2/ha/year as against 42.4 tons CO2/ha/year for tropical rainforest. The root network of the oil palm improves on soil conservation rather than erosion. The fact that most plantations are planted with cover crop means that the soil is well conserved against erosion.

Key stages in the oil palm production chain and the impacts they can have on both the environment and the society

A. Land acquisition

The cultivation of oil palm is dependent on many natural resources, human resources and ecological processes that interlink them. Oil palm producers are seeking for good soils, appropriate climatic conditions, water resources and manpower and since few trees are planted per hectare (143/ha), companies need vast areas of land for cultivation. The use of vast areas of land for the cultivation of oil palm may necessitate the destruction of ecological niches and human settlement. The oil palm is an industrial crop and there are certain limits to achieve in order to make the crop profitable. For an oil palm mill to be profitable, it has to operate at full capacity. Depending on its size and plantation productivity, an oil palm mill needs to be supplied with FFB from a plantation between 4000 ha – 10 000 ha. All companies investing in such an enterprise would be impatient to pay back loans acquired from backs in the shortest possible time, thus they shall be looking for the most fertile lands with a suitable weather. Unfortunately, these areas have early occupants known as indigenes who are undertaking traditional agriculture and if the problem of land acquisition is not properly done, it may lead to conflicts in the long run. These fertile areas are the ones having the majority of HCV because of the availability of food and water. If the principles of HCV protection are not well implemented, then there shall be loss of flora and fauna of great importance.

A series of measures have been prescribed for companies investing on vast areas of land especially on oil palm. These are known as the principles and indicators for the sustainable production of oil palm. It concerns all aspects of the development of plantations including oil palm plantations. All legal issues relating to land acquisition, land use title and plantation establish permit should be transparently and the documents should be made available to the public. Negotiations are expected to be held between traditional or indigenous people and the companies aiming to establish the plantations in order to seek their free, prior and informed consent. Environmental and social impact assessment studies should be carried out as according to the principles of sustainable oil palm plantation establishment. This will explore the possible negative and positive social and environmental impacts made with the participation of the communities. Companies should also draw up a plan and make it public which outlines the type of corporate support to be given to local communities including the construction of farm to market roads, construction of schools and health centres and the award of scholarships to outstanding under privileged student from the local communities. Environmental monitoring in the plantations and its surroundings should be permanent and its reports should also be made public. These reports are an evaluation based on the principles and criteria for sustainable oil palm plantation establishment, applicable local and ratified international laws and regulations.

Oil palm companies should take all the measures mentioned above seriously especially because they shall be the principal determinant of companies' production and productivity in the long run. Companies should note this! Today it is easy to obtain land through the intervention of officials of the powerful centralised governments, especially in countries ruled principally by decrees. BUT! The world is fast changing and countries are becoming more and more democratic with power going directly into the hands of the local people. This time is nearby when the Police, Gendarmes and military shall respect the law and the rights of the people. The people will be the ones deciding for the uniform men and not the reverse. If law shall prevail at that era, then most of the contracts shall be re-written or simply abrogated leading to huge loss in investments. If law does not prevail at that time, communities shall impose their jungle justice on plantation sites and staffs. Therefore, these conflicts shall not only lead to loss of material invested but also to loss in human life.

Although we are not yet at that dream era, there are still some consequences that do affect plantation production and productivity when the company has unsettled conflicts with the local communities or indigenes. This is related to fruit theft in oil palm plantations. All major oil palm companies in Cameroon are facing this problem at this present moment. The theft phenomenon has moved companies to reconvert oil palm plantations into banana and rubber plantations that are less vulnerable to theft. Some plantations have been abandoned because thieves collect the all yield. The companies are presently spending millions of CFA on security but it is also known that these security thugs are usually not unconnected to oil palm theft cases. The oil palm is an invulnerable crop in terms of agro climatology but is a very vulnerable crop with relation to anthropological aspects. This means that although the oil palm can tolerate most environmental inadequacies, it is very attractive and to thieves. This is because thieves can easily recognise when the oil palm is ready for harvest and its fruit has a readily available local market. The oil palm can be refined easily at home by local villages without necessitating expensive technologies. The crude palm oil CPO is consumed in Cameroon directly without prior refining. Most popular traditional dishes in Cameroon use oil palm in this form.

B. Plantation upkeep

Plantation upkeep involves the management of all the aspects contributing to actual yield. These aspects include pest and disease control, appropriate leaf pruning, weed management and fertilisation application. In industrial plantations, most of the field operations are intensive based. Pest control needs large amounts of chemicals in all forms. These chemicals that are mostly inorganic in nature are used to control insects such as leaf miners and Oryctes. Without the use of such chemicals, actual yield of oil palm plantations will diminish seriously. These chemicals may have lethal effects on other organisms to which the oil palm is a non-host. It may also destroy beneficial insects such as pollinators and other useful soil microorganisms. Since most of these chemicals have a wide range of activity and a long lasting persistence, they can be leached into the soil and further into running water. This is harmful for aquatic life and also to those living in the downstream of plantations. An appropriate Integrated Pest Management IPM technique should be applied to control pests and diseases. Best management practices in oil palm plantations will considerably reduce damage caused to surrounding flora and fauna in oil palm plantation. The use of organic manure from waste bunches and palm oil mill effluent as fertiliser and for soil structure improvement should be considered. Weed control should involve the use of cover crops during plantation establishment. Cattle can be used to graze in oil palm plantation in order to control weeds. The cover crop species suitable for such plantations should come from the grasses family such as *Brachiaria spp* which doubles as animal forage. There should be less prophylactic use of agrochemicals.

C. Milling

FFB that is harvested in the plantations is processed in the palm oil mills. In this process, CPO is obtained from FFB. CPO represents 20 – 25% of the total FFB tonnage and the remainder is waste products. This process also produces palm oil mill effluent POME. POME is a mixture of oil and water. POME can cause loss in aquatic life if it is discharged into streams because it modifies the temperature and limits the amount of oxygen in streams. Best Management Practices are available to recycle POME to organic manure and reusable water.

Best Management Practices in oil palm production

Soil conservation

- Conservation of soil, water air and biodiversity
- Enhancing the carbon sink of the soil and crop
- Use empty bunches as mulch against evapo-transpiration, for weed control and organic manure.
- Maintain soft weeds in inter rows and epiphytes on tree trunks including nectar producing plants for insects

Biodiversity

- After carrying out inventorial studies to know the constitution of the area, a biodiversity management plan has to be drawn and well implemented which will include the creation of sanctuaries and conservation zones for High Conservation Value (HCV) Species, wildlife corridors and native tree species
- Avoid using pesticides with high environmental persistence which can cause damage to both fauna and flora
- Avoid prophylactic pesticide sprays but encourage spot-specific sprays to reduce eco-balance disruption

Production

- Use high yielding and productive varieties that can minimise input and optimise yields.

- Plant cover crop at appropriate rates for maximum soil cover, nitrogen fixation, erosion control and organic matter build up.
- Use adapted varieties in order to exploit the variation due to genotype X environment.

Post harvest

- Maintain short harvest rounds (at least 24 turns/year) in order to avoid loss of fruits and fruit rot.
- Ensure high industrial extraction capacities for both CPO and PKO.
- Treat POME effectively and convert it to fertiliser to be used in the field.
- Reduce emission of GHG.

Other sustainability issues

1. Respect of international regulations concerning High Conservation Values HCV areas, criteria developed by the International Financial Corporation IFC, including international conventions such as the United Nations Convention on Biological Diversity UN CBD, the Convention on International Trade in Endangered Species CITES, and the UN Framework convention on Climate Change (UNFCC).
2. Government regulation. The creation of an oil palm hub in Cameroon will obviously call for conflicts that the present legal dispositions may not handle in full. All loopholes in existing regulations have to be covered to ensure that the production of oil

palm in Cameroon does not compromise peace and future existence of mankind. Government regulation should ensure that;

i. All land attributions for plantation establishments should have Free, Prior and Informed Consent (FPIC) of the indigenes. This requires that the indigenous peoples participate in all negotiations leading to the attribution of land, receive benefits, compensation and rights to due process at least equivalent to that which any landowner with full legal title to the land would be entitled to in the case of commercial development on their land.

ii. Companies do not expand above the limits of their land concessions and that the land attributed to them is used for the intended purpose and not just for timber exploitation.

iii. Conflicts with local communities in already existing plantations should be resolved as soon as they arise.

iv. Workers' conditions should be in line with the labour code and other international regulations such as the ILO.

v. Environmental inspection should be done routinely by competent agencies and defaulters sanctioned according to the law. Issues related to pesticide use, POME and other industrial discharges must respect environmental norms.

vi. Companies should practice best management practices.

vii. National regulations including international treaties such as CBD, Cartegena Protocol, should be respected.

How to prevent environmental degradation, social conflicts and economic loss in oil palm plantation establishments

1. No protected-forest conversion for oil palm.

2. There must be no use of fire for land clearing.

3. Conflicts with local communities must be resolved in a way that respects their rights before any expansion of palm oil plantations can take place.

4. Conflicts with local communities on existing plantations must be resolved and the rights of those communities must be respected.

5. Companies engaged in oil palm production, investment or processing must obey the UN norms for multinationals on human rights and labour conditions, and obey national and international human rights and labour laws.

6. Companies operating palm oil plantations must minimise their impact on the environment through good management practices. These should include (but not be limited to):
   - Obeying all relevant Government regulations e.g. on disposal of wastewater.
   - Use of integrated pest management.
   - Significant reduction in the use of pesticides and transparency in the amount of pesticides use.
   - Recycling of Palm Oil Mill Effluent (POME)

7. Companies must establish a mechanism for airing the complaints and redressing the problems of impacted communities, workers, farmers and other affected stakeholders.

8. There must be a regular evaluation of all permits given for oil palm exploitation. The evaluation should investigate:

- Whether companies really use the land in the way they stated they would (e.g. in the case of logging/ oil palm companies, whether the companies did develop oil palm plantations as they said they would, or whether they just logged the forest).

- Whether or not companies expanded outside the boundaries of the concession areas they were granted.

- Whether companies issued with oil palm permits planted oil palm within the time limit stated on the licence.

- How much land has been converted as a result of the issuance of oil palm permits and how much land has been abandoned.

9. The Government must facilitate the resolution of conflicts on oil palm plantations; particularly:

- Prior Informed Consent (PIC) with local communities is needed before any further land conversion takes place.

- Communities impacted by palm oil must have open access to company representatives and the government in order to negotiate their position,

- Communities impacted by oil palm must have open access to the necessary information about the impacts and future expansion plans of oil palm companies.

10. Central government regulations on palm oil plantations and Cameroonian labour laws need to be reformed so that the reliance of the oil palm sector on daily labourers is ended. Every employee on a

plantation must have a contract and basic labour rights, including (but not limited to):

- The right to form independent labour Unions

- The rights for women workers to have maternity leave

- The right to a living wage without working overtime

- The right to work without fear of violence

- Bonuses for workers in proportion to company profits

11. The Government must enforce regulations against the use of violence by companies on the people.

Procedure for new plantings

Recommendation for new plantings should be based on the successful completion of the following 5-step process;

1. Independent Environmental and Social Impact Assessment (ESIA) of the area concerned including all primary forests, local peoples land, HCV and peat soils.

2. An implementation plan based on the ESIA assessments respecting primary forests and local peoples' land.

3. Verification or field audit by a certification body to review and confirm that the assessments were comprehensive, and in compliance with existing regulations.

4. Public notification should be carried out to inform the general public especially the affected populations at least 30 days prior to land preparation.

5. All conflicts should be resolved as they arise.

If a majority of these rules are observed, then oil palm can be sustainably produced in Cameroon. The economy will grow and employment shall rise. Incomes will increase and the trade balance shall gradually turn from deficit to surplus. Socially, there will be less crime in the neighbourhood.

A not for profit apolitical and non – trade unionist organization registered under the Cameroonian laws and constitution.

Head Office

Batoke, PMB 77 Limbe

Tel: +237 697781394

South West Region

Republic of Cameroon

Objectives

1. To promote and facilitate the implementation of RSPO principles in Central Africa.

2. Create a database on suitable land (excluding HCVs and protected areas) for the development of major plantation crops.

3. To contribute to the protection of the environment especially marine, fresh water and reserves adjacent to farms and plantations.

4. Mount projects for sustainable plantation development

5. Promote sustainable plantation crops development.

6. To raise public and political awareness on the necessity of encouraging sustainable agriculture as a means of poverty alleviation.;

Reg No. RC/2016/A/3133

CAmINdo is an international consultancy on plantation crops (Oil Palm, Rubber, Cocoa, coffee, Jatropha, Pepper, Fruit trees, coconut..) with high profile and experienced experts drawn across Africa and Asia. CAmINdo collaborates with renowned laboratories, prominent agricultural universities, Agricultural research institutions Agro – industries and Small farmers.

It has been noticed that many investors have wasted money on failed agricultural projects. Several factors accounted for these failures, among others; unsuitable planting site, poor planting material, unsustainable cropping methods, poor fertilizer application, low yields and insufficient knowledge on market opportunities.

We provide individuals and agro industrial companies efficient, adapted and innovative methods including research and training for a successful agricultural project.

Head Office
Eamil: camindo@gmail.com
BP 14562 Bastos Yaoundé. Tel: +237 672657455
RCCM: RC/YAO/2016/A/3133

Mission
CAmINdo accompanies individual investors and agro industries to practice efficient and sustainable agricultural production

Activities
Plantation development
- Land Acquisition
- Land suitability studies
- Rapid Soil Appraisal
- Land preparation to planting

Farm management
- Seed production and nursery management
- Seed/variety recommendation
- Foliar Survey
- Fertilizer recommendations
- Pests and diseases survey
- Pesticide recommendation

Modernization of Production process
- Provision of innovative production technologies
- Provision of adapted technologies

Training
- Short term training of management staff
- Refresher courses for plantation staff
- Intensified on-farm training for new graduates from agricultural schools and faculties
- Placement of trained staff to plantations.

Impact Assessment Studies

www.ingramcontent.com/pod-product-compliance
Lightning Source LLC
Chambersburg PA
CBHW081552220526
45468CB00013B/2277

* 9 7 8 1 7 2 3 9 2 5 8 5 6 *